guide

MAXXI

**Museo nazionale
delle arti
del XXI secolo**

Electa

Guide edited by
Sofia Bilotta
Alessio Rosati

www.electaweb.com

Membership Program
Founding Donors
I live MAXXI

MAXXI stands for National Museum of the Arts of the twenty-first century. It is one of Italy's leading public museums, the first one devoted to contemporary creativity, to art and to architecture.
For many centuries, Italian art and architecture constituted the avant-garde, a model for the Western world's creativity, with the awe-inspiring monuments of Classical Rome, the work of Cimabue and Giotto in the Middle Ages, Masaccio and Brunelleschi in the Renaissance, who were followed by Raphael and Michelangelo, and, lastly, that of Bernini and Borromini in the Baroque Age.
The MAXXI follows in the footsteps of the great Italian artistic tradition, its goal to become a centre of excellence where manifold forms of expression, productivity and creation all converge and blend together. Art has always foreshadowed modes and thinking, experimentation in and the innovation of languages and messages. The forms and lines of the MAXXI's architecture express all these things by way of a daring, experimental building, set amidst Rome's topography and even its history, completely permeable to the contemporary. Hence, the MAXXI is a cultural institute conceived as a great workshop of contemporary culture, a dynamic one, evolving, sensitive to the changes and conflicts of the society we live in. A society where art plays an essential role, because it is an iconic and symbolic language, bestowed thus with a comprehensibility that is superior to the written or spoken word, contributing to the understanding of worlds and cultures otherwise extraneous and potentially in contrast, and favouring the healing of reciprocal differences. Art and architecture also constitute the essential components of how a country is viewed abroad, accompanying its image in the rest of the world. They express a country's cultural vitality, its penchant for renewal, its inclination towards creative and original research. Italian art and architecture are this country's expression and narrative, capable of conveying not just the concept known as *made in Italy*, the Italian product, but something farther-reaching and more complex that we might call the Italian lifestyle, "il vivi italiano" – the Italian way of life.
From this standpoint, the MAXXI is like an antenna transmitting Italy's contents to the outside world while, in turn, receiving the flux of international culture from the outside. Hence, on the one hand it projects outwards towards the world, while on the other, it expresses the essence of that highly unique culture that was born right here in Italy.

Pio Baldi
President of the Fondazione MAXXI

This Guide was written to provide the reader/visitor with an easy tool for getting around the museum's complex and evocative spaces, a handbook of sorts through Zaha Hadid's architecture and the museum's collections, presented along with a partial but significant overview of the research being conducted in Italy and abroad.
A museum of its own time, the MAXXI is a dynamic and intricate reality, not just an extraordinary building designed to house a wealth of artworks, and to host events and public services. It is a vital cultural centre, energized by research activity and documentation, exhibitions and conservation, patronage and the promotion of contemporary art and architecture. In the Guide, a visit to the MAXXI is organised topographically. The texts and images accompany the reader in his or her discovery of the museum and its architecture, space after space, artwork after artwork, unveiling materials and techniques, specifying dimensions and features – much like a hypertext through which to embark on a very personal cultural path. The pages of the Guide devoted to the exhibition complex and its collections are followed by one last section that lists the many services and facilities readily available to the public, which contribute to making the MAXXI a cultural pole of knowledge, recreation and entertainment. The book ends with a few of the highlights from the history of the architectural project and museum, both of which have so greatly contributed to changing the urban and cultural identity of the Flaminio quarter and the city of Rome.

We hope that your visit to the museum, in the company of this Guide, will be an opportunity to plunge into a unique and stimulating dimension, an experience, through the artworks and spaces, that will be both satisfying and exciting, and that will take place each time you visit the two museums, or perhaps just stop in the plaza located right in front. The MAXXI is perpetually in motion, alternating exhibitions and cultural initiatives, promoting a variety of events and activities so that the public will always have a reason to go back. And thanks to its open spaces, the area is also an urban campus for socialization and recreation to be experienced and shared by all.
In the words of Zaha Hadid, to whom the idea for this extraordinary project is due, it is a place where *"architecture must offer pleasure, when people enter an architectural space, they should experience a feeling of well-being and harmony..."*

And this is exactly what we wish for our visitors.

Margherita Guccione
Director of MAXXI Architecture

Anna Mattirolo
Director of MAXXI Art

Table of Contents

"Our proposal offers a quasi-urban field, a world to dive into rather than a building as signature object. The campus is organised and navigated on the basis of directional drifts and the distribution of densities rather than key points. This is indicative of the character of the centre as a whole: porous, immersive, a field space."

Zaha Hadid

Visiting the museum

The MAXXI's architecture rises up from a daring and original idea for a museum space: flux and force fields, imaginary trajectories traced out by its visitors take shape in the architect's mind and are materialised in space, volumes that project into the void, walls that curve around and fold upon themselves, unexpected openings to the exterior and lookouts onto the full height of the interior characterise the path inside the museum and draw the visitor into a complex and intriguing physical and mental experience.

A challenge to our way of perceiving things and to the traditional idea of an exhibition space, a place where the art and architecture of our time can be experienced in a new way.

The old idea of a predetermined path is set aside in favour of a multiplicity of possible spatial criss-crossings, without the visitor ever needing to retrace his or her steps.

The MAXXI's big numbers

Total surface area of the lot
29,000 sq m
Exterior space
19,640 sq m
Interior space
21,200 sq m
Total exhibition area
10,000 sq m
Facilities (auditorium,
library, media library, café,
restaurant, etc.)
6,200 sq m

Level 0

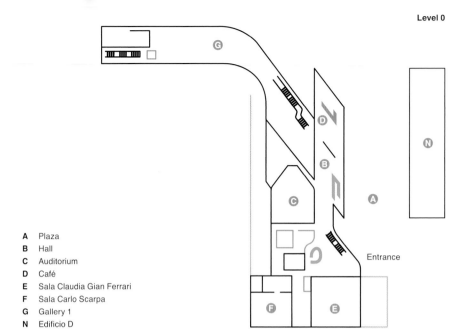

A   Plaza
B   Hall
C   Auditorium
D   Café
E   Sala Claudia Gian Ferrari
F   Sala Carlo Scarpa
G   Gallery 1
N   Edificio D

Entrance

Level 1

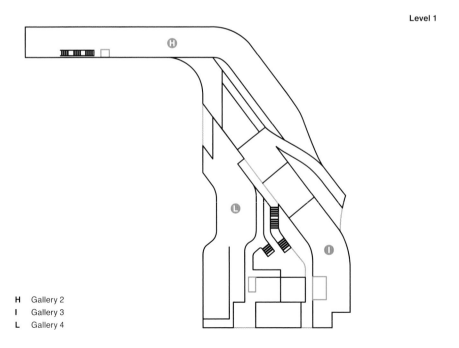

H   Gallery 2
I   Gallery 3
L   Gallery 4

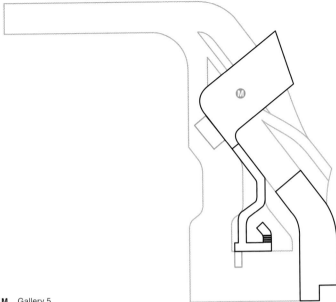

M Gallery 5

 PLAZA

Conceived as an open and liveable urban space, you can reach the museum plaza from either Via Guido Reni or Via Masaccio. A walkway connects the two streets and fulfils the urban development plan of 1909, which, because of the construction of the Montello barracks, never actually materialised. By occupying the entire area, the barracks structure modified the neighbourhood's typical orthogonal plan, an impassible interruption rising up between the two major arteries. The citizens can now reclaim this space, more as an urban location than a museum site.

❶
Gallery 5 is a 9-m long cantilevered volume that projects out above the plaza

The maximum height of the building is 22.70 m

Ⓑ HALL

The full height space of the hall is an intricate geometrical design of stairways and walls made from unfaced concrete, an element that plays a prominent role in the building. By looking upwards from here you soon perceive the existence of a maze-like network of paths and trajectories; explored progressively, they reveal the building's extraordinary spatial mechanism, which is difficult to comprehend on first sight. The heart of the space, and the starting point for the visitor, is the **information and ticket counter**. This portion of Zaha Hadid's MAXXI was grafted onto the block of the former Montello barracks, a two-level industrial structure built in the early twentieth century and converted into a museum, recognisable from the façade overlooking Via Guido Reni.

Hall 520 sq m

Clearly visible on the unfaced concrete is the further pouring of reinforced concrete at a height of 10.53 m.

The MAXXI's unfaced **concrete**, devoid of cladding, is a self-compacting mixture, the result of an experiment performed directly on the construction site. Very fine aggregates in the mixture give the concrete a silky touch and cause it to reflect light. Circular holes covered by cement plugs house the reinforcing steel bars of the formwork.

The **counter made from GRC** (Glass Reinforced Concrete) is a shell cast and mounted on a metal frame, and finished with a layer of gelcoat.

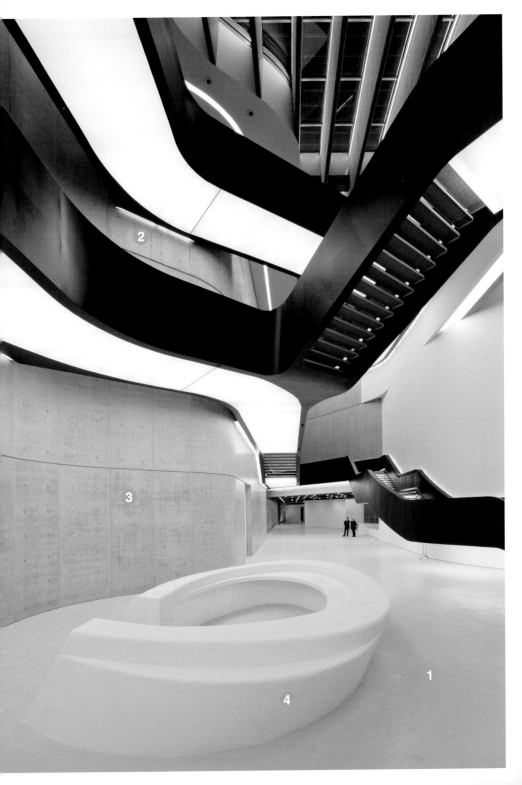

Ⓒ AUDITORIUM

To the left of the hall, if you head in the direction of Gallery 1, you'll come to the auditorium. The space features wenge parquet flooring and a lighting system for the ceiling and back wall that translates the need for completely artificial lighting into a refined geometrical design, an ever-changing lacework of bright shapes. The seating is a nod to the MAXXI's essential, razor-edged architecture. The space is used for viewing, film festivals, conferences and lectures.

❶
Auditorium 284 sq m

The main floor has seats for up to 240 spectators

HALL
CAFÉ

If you return to the hall and walk towards the café, you'll find another counter where you can pick up an audio-visual guide and book some of the educational activities. This counter, which is also made from GRC, projects into space like a ship's prow. Its sharp-edged, dynamic lines follow those of the architecture. The ceiling replicates the auditorium's lighting system. The glass partitions on the left lead into the MAXXI Architecture area.

❶ Hall 290 sq m

❷ The counter where audio-visual guides are stored, and where educational activities can be booked

❸ Café 204 sq m

❹ A wall-drawing by Sol LeWitt was made in the hall.

Ⓔ SALA CLAUDIA GIAN FERRARI

At the opposite end of the hall, broad arches on the ground floor lead into the Sala Claudia Gian Ferrari, a room featuring bare, homogeneously regular architecture that reminds us of its former industrial use. Owing to its smaller size, the flexibility of the space, which can be divided by partitions, and its position, which is off-centre in relation to the exhibition galleries, the room is ideal for hosting temporary exhibitions.
The Educational Department's Teaching Laboratory and the Conference Room are both located on the first floor of what was once the industrial building.

Sala Claudia Gian Ferrari
420 sq m

The MAXXI's spatulated cement **floor** was made artisanally. Large spatulas were used to achieve a homogeneous effect and any human trace is imperceptible. The surface is formally characterised by the fact that it's joint-free.

The **cast-iron columns**, cast in 1907, are 5.97 m high.

F SALA CARLO SCARPA

Returning to the hall and walking past the bookstore and lift you come to the Sala Carlo Scarpa. The room is built from the block of the former barracks, where four concrete parallelepipeds support the floor of Gallery 4. This space, like the previous one characterised by simple, even geometries and vast windows that allow natural light to filter in, is dedicated to MAXXI Architecture's collection of photography.

Sala Carlo Scarpa 230 sq m

Each **pier** has a base measuring 1.00 × 0.30 m and is 6.00 m high.

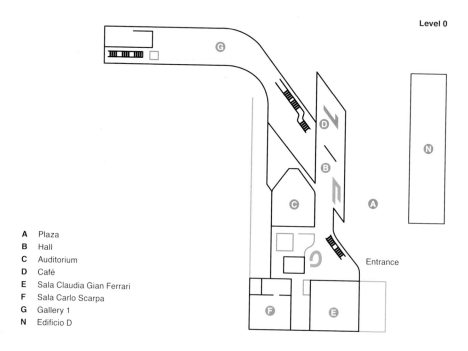

Level 0

A Plaza
B Hall
C Auditorium
D Café
E Sala Claudia Gian Ferrari
F Sala Carlo Scarpa
G Gallery 1
N Edificio D

Entrance

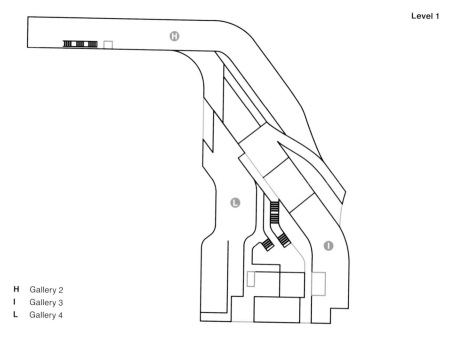

Level 1

H Gallery 2
I Gallery 3
L Gallery 4

MAXXI Architecture
Museum of modern and contemporary architecture

Ⓖ GALLERY 1

Gallery 1 hosts the Architecture Museum and its Archives Centre. After going past the glass wall at the museum entrance you'll enter the MAXXI's second full height space. The stairway on the right leads to Galleries 2 and 3 devoted to art. This is the only exhibition space in the museum that is totally artificially lit because its ceiling acts as a support to Gallery 2, located above. The unfaced concrete walls make way for plaster wallboards. The gallery is conceived as a continuum, enlivened by the movement of the wall-partition. The traditional and static concept of the exhibition hall is done away with, and reshaped into a dynamic environment, a metaphor for the spatial and cultural context of our day. Inside the galleries, works making up the permanent collection for the two art and architecture museums are displayed on a rotational basis, meaning that they are never mounted the same way.

Gallery 1 1,140 sq m

The use of **reinforced plaster wallboards** makes it easy to hang the artworks, which can also be easily replaced if so required by the various displays. A 60-cm cavity between the outer cement wall and the inner plaster wallboard houses all of the technical equipment. The climate control system is located in open ventilation grids at the bottom or top of the walls.

For the **artificial lighting system** fluorescent lamps are recessed into the double ceiling and shielded with layers of Barrisol®.

The wall-partition is 5.85 m high.

THE MUSEUM OF ARCHITECTURE

THE ARCHITECTURE ARCHIVES CENTRE
Study and consultation room

In line with the MAXXI's cultural mission, the Museum of Architecture is an open, dynamic international institute that makes full use of the most advanced tools to disseminate a knowledge of architecture and bear witness to its role in society. The Museum's activities unfold along two distinct but complementary courses of action, with the aim of presenting modern and contemporary architecture to the public as well as to those who work in the field. The first course of action is of a historical-critical nature and is limited to twentieth-century architecture, presented here by way of retrospective exhibitions devoted to eminent figures or specific twentieth-century topics, encouraging study and thinking aimed at learning about and rediscovering its value. The second course of action is more innovative and experimental, and entirely devoted to the ongoing debate and emerging themes of the contemporary, with special interest in young architects and the international scene; its aim is to inspire and motivate the public and those who work in the field to encounter the ideas and spaces of the future. All of MAXXI Architecture's exhibitions are temporary; this allows the museum to overcome any limits in space or time, and offers its visitors ever-growing and wide-ranging opportunities to understand architecture. It is the purpose of the publications that accompany the exhibitions to bear witness to what has taken place over the years, and to provide valuable sources of information for all those who are interested. The museum's collections are continually expanding and displayed on a rotational basis in its galleries; all of the material housed in MAXXI Architecture is available to the public for consultation in the Archives Centre.

MAXXI's Architecture Archives Center collects, conserves and manages the museum's collections, and also favours their promotion and dissemination. Included in the collection are the personal archives of such eminent twentieth-century architects as Carlo Scarpa, Aldo Rossi and Pier Luigi Nervi. Alongside sketches, drawings, models, photographs and professional documents that once belonged to these authors are materials presented for the architectural competitions organised by the Board of Directors for Landscape, the Fine Arts, Architecture and Contemporary Art and by the Italian Ministry of Culture. This includes projects for the MAXXI itself, those related to the institute's mission to promote architecture and, lastly, those destined to young architects. The Architecture Museum's special collections also contain the results of activities and events – exhibitions, commissions, laboratories – that derive from the MAXXI's own cultural and research projects, together with prototypes, design objects and objects representing industrial production. All of these materials, available in digital format in a dedicated space located in the Archives Centre, can easily be consulted by the public.

FROM THE COLLECTIONS
OF THE MUSEUM
OF ARCHITECTURE

Six Italian masters of the twentieth century

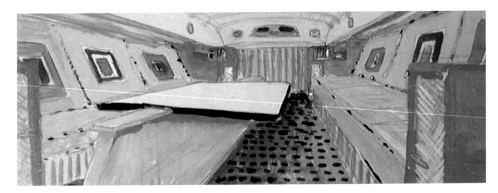

Carlo Scarpa (Venice 1906 – Sendai, Japan 1978)
Architect, artist and designer, Carlo Scarpa is considered to be one of the most fascinating figures on the twentieth-century architectural scene. Most of his activity involved exhibition assembly, monument restoration and designs for shops and private homes. The archive was acquired in 2001 and is prevalently technical and architectural in nature, documenting the gamut of the architect's activity from 1927 to 1978. Drawings, sketches and etchings, books and photographic documentation, some of which unpublished, testify to Scarpa's ceaseless formal and functional research and his painstaking attention to detail.

Carlo Scarpa
Project for the interior design of the Yacht "Asta", 1935, MAXXI Architecture collection

Enrico Del Debbio (Carrara 1891 – Rome 1973)
One of the most eminent architects active in
Rome between the 1920s and the 1970s,
Enrico Del Debbio built the city's Foro Italico
sports complex, the Italian Foreign Affairs
Ministry, the Swimming Stadium and the Faculty
of Architecture in Rome, among others.
The Enrico Del Debbio archive contains material
produced by the architect over the course of his
lengthy professional career, which chiefly
unfolded in Rome, and stretched from 1920 to
1968. In addition to the actual architectural plans,
the collection includes photographs, letters and
a portion of Del Debbio's early artistic production
– oil paintings, charcoal drawings, pastels
and watercolours.

Enrico Del Debbio
*Academy of Physical Education,
Foro Mussolini*, 1927, MAXXI
Architecture collection

Sergio Musmeci (Rome 1926 – 1981)
Sergio Musmeci was awarded a degree in civil
and aeronautical engineering, and is considered
to be one of the most daring structuralists of the
twentieth century. Alongside his collaborative
work with some of the greatest Italian architects
of the twentieth century, he designed some very
complex structures, such as the viaduct over the
Basento River in Potenza and the bridge over the
Via Appia Antica in Rome. Musmeci's personal
archive was acquired in 2003, and it contains
material documenting his professional work in
Italy and abroad, and his scientific research into
the themes of formal structure. The archive also
includes notes, lesson plans, teaching material
and a large collection of letters.

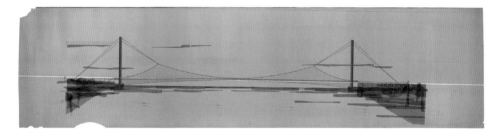

Sergio Musmeci
*Project for a Bridge over the Strait
of Messina*, 1969, in collaboration
with Zenaide Zanini, MAXXI
Architecture collection

Pier Luigi Nervi (Sondrio 1891 – Rome 1979)
Pier Luigi Nervi was awarded a degree in civil engineering and devoted his entire career to architecture and the calculation of architectural structures. As a result of his great interest in the potential of reinforced concrete, from 1920 he held a dual role as architect and constructor. The large number of documents – acquired in 2004 – bear witness to Pier Luigi Nervi's work from 1920 to 1980, and they attest to the architectural activity carried out by his firm on technological experimentation with reinforced concrete structures throughout the world, his scientific and teaching activity and his relations with other major figures in the twentieth-century realms of architecture, culture and business.

Pier Luigi Nervi
"Palazzetto" Sports Stadium, Rome, 1960, MAXXI Architecture collection

Aldo Rossi (Milan 1931 – 1997)
An architect and an architectural theoretician,
Aldo Rossi was one of the most eminent figures
of Italian architecture in the post-Second World
War period. Throughout his career his work as
an architect went hand in hand with research
and teaching, and he was the first Italian
architect to win the Pritzker Prize, in 1990.
The architect's archive was acquired in 2002,
and comprises models, projects and drawings
relating to architecture, as well as drawings of
artistic value that accompanied the different
stages in design. Additional documents
of a technical nature, writings, audio-visual
recordings provide a wide-ranging view of Aldo
Rossi's professional, teaching, scientific and
cultural activity.

Aldo Rossi
*Competition entry for the Marburger
Museum*, Marburg, 1987, MAXXI
Architecture collection

Vittorio De Feo (Naples 1928 – Rome 2002)
Vittorio De Feo's idea of architecture is
wide-ranging artistic research where painting,
sculpture and literature are all combined, and his
penchant for experimentation in his work can be
seen in the great number of projects developed
in over fifty years of activity. Besides his work as
an architect and a university lecturer, De Feo
conducted significant historical studies on
Russian architecture, Robert Venturi and
Baroque art and culture. The De Feo archive,
which comprises graphic representations, notes,
photographs, slides and models, also includes an
invaluable collection of bibliographic material.

Vittorio De Feo
Marian Oratory in Deruta (PG),
1995, MAXXI Architecture collection

ⓗ GALLERY 2

From Gallery 1, you can take the stairs or lift to reach Gallery 2. The first half of the area is devoted to MAXXI Architecture, the other half to MAXXI Art. The blank walls again make way for plaster wallboard. The natural light that filters through the complex roofing system is a key feature of the museum. The flight of cement fins that run parallel to one another, and are perpendicular to the gallery, act as a guide here, and underscore the direction of the path, heightening and emphasising the project's fluid, sinuous lines.

Gallery 2 1,290 sq m

The gallery measures a linear length of 147 m

The height of the wall-partition is 12.60 m

The height of the floor is 6.60 m

The segments made of GRC that support the transparent **roof** house the artificial lighting system and all of the mechanisms required to activate the brise-soleil. This is what regulates the natural light in the spaces inside depending on the season, time of day and weather; if required, the gallery can be completely darkened. Moveable panels that may be required by a specific exhibition can be hung from tracks located underneath the segments. Outside, on the transparent roof, a glass covering and steel grids protect the interior by blocking out the sunlight, and avoid overheating in summer.

Four major figures
of twenty-first-century
international architecture

Alessandro Anselmi
*Project for a mixed-use building
near the San Pietro train station,*
Rome, 2002, MAXXI Architecture
collection

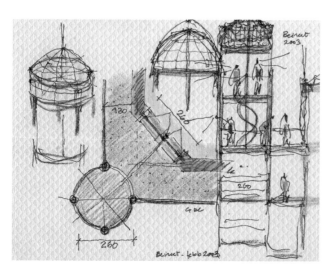

Giancarlo De Carlo
Project for residences in Beirut,
2003, MAXXI Architecture collection

Zaha Hadid
Model for the Centre for contemporary arts, Rome, 1999, MAXXI Architecture collection

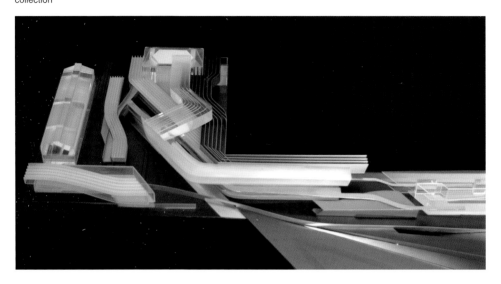

Toyo Ito
Model for the TOD'S building, Omotesando, Tokyo, Japan, 2004, MAXXI Architecture collection

The photography and architecture collection

At the present time, MAXXI Architecture's photography collection contains 1,000 fine art photographs acquired from 2003 by way of projects commissioned as part of research programmes and studies conducted on Italy's landscape, urban scenario and architecture. The architecture museum's lead line is photography: this is because of the role it plays as a medium of communication for the presentation of the physical arrangement of space, inevitably lying outside the museum. But also because of the authorial dimension of photographic research, poised somewhere between documentation and critical, subjective and unilateral interpretation of space and reality. Accordingly, the research conducted made use of photography as both a means and an end: as a means because it is a tool that records the state of the country in terms of its changing landscape, aimed at documenting and interpreting, constructing memory, foreshadowing development and forming awareness. At the same time, apart from the results of such research, as photography is also a physical object, it was also the very goal of the commissions, whose purpose was to acquire quality work for the museum's permanent collections. Photographs that are acquired in this way infringe upon their purely (albeit useful) documentary purpose and acquire additional poetic and aesthetic value that goes beyond the departure zone and spreads into other fields to produce unexpected effects that can help us understand what's happening around us.
The choice of using a commission as a strategy rather than directly acquiring works already on the market fulfils another of the museum's missions: to act as a culture-producing machine, nurturing and encouraging the artists' work, developing a relationship with them so that their activity becomes linked to the cultural events promoted by the MAXXI. Naturally, the selection of photographers in MAXXI Architecture's collection is not an exhaustive one: it is an ongoing collection, which will be expanded with works by other authors – either emerging artists or ones whose fame is already well-established – who are a part of the vast and many-hued fine art photography scene.

Mimmo Jodice
Genoa, la sopraelevata, 2002,
MAXXI Architecture photography
collection

Massimo Vitali
Palermo, Mondello Beach, 2007,
MAXXI Architecture photography
collection

Livello 1

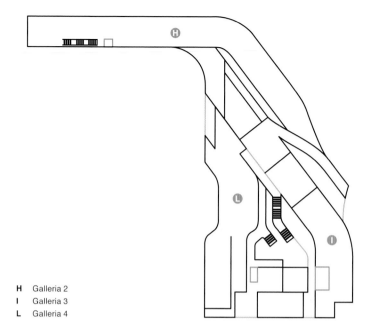

H   Galleria 2
I   Galleria 3
L   Galleria 4

Livello 2

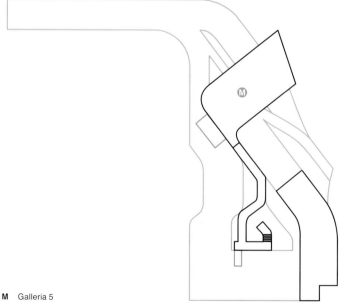

M   Galleria 5

MAXXI Art

Halfway down Gallery 2, where MAXXI
Architecture ends, the wall on the right opens
onto Gallery 3. This is where MAXXI Art begins.
The visitor can choose to continue along Gallery
2, or change direction. The spaces flow into
one another uninterruptedly, like paths
criss-crossing in the woods.

Maurizio Mochetti
Calotte di fiberglass con elastico –
Oggetto polimerico, 1966-67,
installation, elasticized cotton,
fiberglass, room-size. Courtesy
Maurizio Mochetti

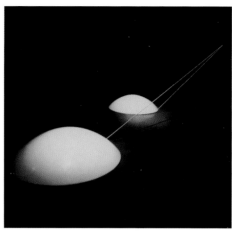

Massimo Bartolini
Mixing parfums, 2000, installation,
illuminated revolving door, jasmine
essence, room-size

MAXXI Art and the collection

The idea for the MAXXI derived from a project conceived by the Italian Ministry of Culture as the ideal continuation of the Galleria Nazionale d'Arte Moderna in Rome, whose collections chiefly concern the nineteenth and twentieth centuries and are by now historicised in nature. On the contrary, the MAXXI was conceived as a place that would welcome and experiment with the most up-to-date languages of the arts, a reality that entirely moves in the direction of the future. In order to harmonise and ensure the continuity of the collections in the two institutes, MAXXI Art has established that its acquisitions will begin – more or less and with some flexibility – from the year 2000, without, however, overlooking documentation from the recent past: the last fifty years of art history. Alongside artworks by a generation of artists who were mostly born in the 1960s and 1970s, the presence of a selection of works by the masters helps us to understand the research that has been conducted in Italy in recent years, the relationships, exchanges and mutual influence between figures of very different ages. Thus, comparisons can be made between the works of Mario Merz, Michelangelo Pistoletto, Alighiero Boetti, Giulio Paolini, Gino De Dominicis, those of Stefano Arienti, Bruna Esposito, Massimo Bartolini, Mario Airò, Eva Marisaldi, to name just a few, and of the youngest of them all, Claudia Losi, Giuseppe Gabellone, Stefania Galegati, Francesco Vezzoli. It is the purpose of the MAXXI collection to reveal the wealth and complexity of the national artistic context by tracing its specific features as being deeply rooted in this land, without, however, forgoing evidence from the international scene. The latter aspect is dealt with by the museum along the lines of interpretation that show predilection for artists more closely linked to the Italian context, such artists as Alfredo Jaar, Kiki Smith, Adrian Paci. MAXXI Art currently holds a collection of more than 300 works, a number that is constantly growing thanks to an acquisitions campaign that supports and to a certain extent mirrors the exhibition aspect, by exploiting a number of modalities: acquisitions, direct commissions via awards, competitions and exhibitions, donations and long-term loans. The **Premio per la Giovane Arte Italiana** (4 of these, from 2000 to 2007) added as many as 30 works, realised for this specific purpose, to the museum's collections: to name just a few, *Città ideale* by Liliana Moro and *Climbing* by Vedovamazzei in 2000, *Monologue Patterns (Crisalide)* by Loris Cecchini and *La Terra è troppo grande* by Lara Favaretto, both winners in 2004-05. The competition format has been a very efficient means of monitoring the artistic scene on a national level. The museum, in its role as patron, has promoted and backed the work of younger artists, ensuring their visibility through their participation at the Venice Biennale and exhibitions held in the MAXXI's temporary locations (Edificio D, which currently houses some of the museum's services, was the site of intense exhibition activity from 2003 to 2009). The new **Premio Italia Arte Contemporanea** falls within the legacy of the previous award, and its intention is to constitute a crucial moment in the institutional acknowledgement and international promotion of artists under 45 years of age who have made a significant contribution to artistic research in Italy for about ten years. The **Premio MAXXIduepercento** is an international competition linked to a law passed

William Kentridge
North Pole Map, 2003,
Embroidered silk tapestry
weave, 340 × 390 cm

in 1949 which stated that government-run administrations and all public bodies that have public buildings erected must allot no less than 2% of the project's total estimated cost for the production of works of art. This particular award was actually the first application of the law in Italy, which resulted in Maurizio Mochetti's *Rette di luce nell'iperspazio curvilineo* and Massimo Grimaldi's *Emergency's Paediatric Centre in Port Sudan Supported by MAXXI*, both acquired by the MAXXI collections and displayed in the museum hall and plaza. Private **donations** are another major source of acquisitions for the collection. Claudia Gian Ferrari's donation ensured that the public could admire 58 significant works by such Italian and foreign artists as Charles Avery, Matthew Barney, Gabriele Basilico, Christian Boltanski, Pier Paolo Calzolari, Tony Cragg, Marlene Dumas, William Kentridge, Anselm Kiefer, Ettore Spalletti and Patrick Tuttofuoco. The Museum of Contemporary Art is a dynamic organism that is constantly undergoing change. For it to be able to interpret and communicate the present, it turns metamorphosis into a modus operandi. This explains why the permanent collection is displayed to the public on a rotational basis, with selective criteria that range from a specific subject to the in-depth analysis of the works of a single artist or group of artists, and the consequent ever-changing trajectories for the visitor. The path that leads through the museum spaces is nonetheless marked by a number of fixed environmental installations.

Stefano Arienti
Ciliegio e tulipani, 1991-93, partially erased poster mounted on a panel, 96 × 104 cm, Courtesy Stefano Arienti

Lara Favaretto
La terra è troppo grande, 2005,
video installation, projection room,
partitioning and outer box in Mdf,
video projector, DVD player, b/w
DVD, sound, loop, room-size.
Premio per la Giovane Arte Italiana
2004-05. Courtesy Galleria Franco
Noero, Turin

Vedovamazzei
Climbing, 2000, installation, iron,
crystal, light bulbs, silver fox fur,
diameter 300 cm. Premio per la
Giovane Arte Italiana 2000

Wolfgang Tillmans
Mental Pictures #30, 2000,
cibachrome print, 60 × 51 cm.
Donated by Claudia Gian Ferrari

Armin Linke
*Veduta dell'interno dello Ski Dome
di Tokyo*, 1998

The permanent installations

Widow (2004) by **Anish Kapoor** (Bombay, India 1954) consists in black pvc-coated polyester fabric that was stretched out and fastened to the surrounding walls. The work of this Indian-born British artist is situated at the crossroads between two very different cultural traditions: Western and Eastern. Like many of his other works that incorporate the use of reflecting materials, Kapoor manipulates and provides a shape to the void, drawing the viewer into a visual, spatial and psychic experience with a strong impact. The viewer's eye is attracted to the complex geometry of the container, but while it attempts to penetrate it, it is spurned by its impenetrability. Unable to take up some kind of privileged position, the viewer is forced into a state of continuous instability with the work. The artwork becomes a metaphor for a particular way of approaching and familiarising onself with the world through sensorial perception. The installation is on display in Gallery 1 of the Museum of Architecture.

Anish Kapoor
Widow, 2004, installation, pvc-coated polyester fabric, steel, 4610 × 14630 × 4610 cm. Courtesy Galleria Massimo Minini, Brescia

From the very outset of his career as an exponent of Minimalism **Sol LeWitt** (Hartford, USA 1928 – New York 2007) was accompanied by the forms of Euclidean geometry. *Wall Drawing #375* (1982) is part of a series planned from 1981, when LeWitt began to spend long periods of time in Spoleto, Italy. The artist's encounter with the great frescoed cycles of fifteenth-century Italian art inspired him to reflect on the relationship between painting and the architectural container. Geometrical solids stand out against the surface of the wall and question its two-dimensional nature. In the axonometric representation, the orthogonal lines of the three solids do not converge towards a single vanishing point. The univocal and coherent construction of space is denied in favour of a dialectic perception between real environment and illusionistic space. The logical and rational approach that is required of the viewer moves towards intuition and beyond, towards an ambiguous state that some critics have compared to an experience of immersion akin to mysticism. The work was realised by LeWitt's assistants to a design by the artist and is on display in the Hall.

Sol LeWitt
Wall Drawing #375, 1982,
installation, coloured ink, room-size

Sculture di Linfa (2007) by **Giuseppe Penone**
(Garessio di Cuneo 1947) condenses some of
the subjects and forms of the artist's work in
recent years. The artist has always been
interested in the osmotic relationship between
the human being and nature in their reciprocal
mirroring of one another; the opportunity for the
former to intervene in the development
processes of the latter; art, and especially
sculpture, as a surface for the transit and
accumulation of energies through the material.
The walls of the environment are covered with
bark, which is in turn covered with leather. Skin
on skin, vegetable and animal are merged
together in the indistinct continuity of nature. The
marble pavement features crinkles and reliefs as
if the artist had teased out of the material the
veins of the stone or had discovered the trace of
a brain. At the centre, a long and grooved length
of timber has a resin heart. The tree is the
common thread in this work, a complex
installation that entails sight, touch and smell.
The work is on display in Gallery 4.

Giuseppe Penone
Sculture di linfa, 2007, installation,
wood, leather, resin, Carrara
marble, room-size

From the 1960s to the present: selected works

Mario Merz (Milan 1925 – Turin 2003) first began to work on the "igloo" form in 1968; according to the artist, this environmental construction creates a whole world and the small home, private space and all that is real. In his works Merz used the numerical series elaborated in the thirteenth century by Leonardo Fibonacci, a mathematician from Pisa; in the series each number is the sum of the two numbers that come before (1, 1, 2, 3, 5, 8, 13...) and the relationship between them implies the growth of natural phenomena. In *Senza titolo (Triplo igloo)*, 1984, the Fibonacci series made in neon and the three igloos placed one inside the other allude to the evolution of the cosmos and of man, to the impulses and the vital energies that animate the universe. Because the work is mostly made from a fragile, transparent material like glass, it fosters thought on the precariousness of existence, on the natural, protective instinct, but also on the need to make contact with the outside world.

Mario Merz
Senza titolo (Triplo igloo), 1984-2002, installation, glass, clamps, clay, neon, individual igloos: 300 × 600, 400 × 200, 200 × 100 cm

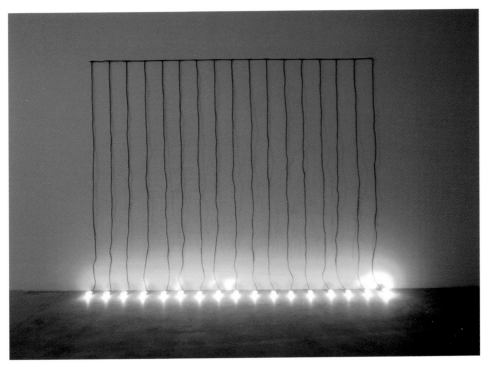

The work of **Michelangelo Pistoletto** (Biella 1933) entitled
Quadro di fili elettrici – Tenda di lampadine (1967) is an ironic
and contemporary rereading of the painting as object. The media
traditionally used for painting are replaced with everyday objects
such as light bulbs and electrical wiring. At the same time,
however, as it is a source of light, the light bulb alludes to a
subject that has always been very successful and extremely
important in painting, the very element of its construction. Arte
Povera, the movement that arose from the mid-1960s and to which
Pistoletto was associated, nurtures the idea of the recycling of
commonly available objects. These artists, known as "poveristi",
rejected consumer society and rapid industrialisation, where art
had become a product for cultural consumption; instead they
practised the dematerialisation of the object, and chose to work
with technologically poor materials.

Michelangelo Pistoletto
*Quadro di fili elettrici – Tenda di
lampadine*, 1967, electrical wiring,
light bulbs, 268 × 440 cm

In the corpus of works by **Alighiero Boetti** (Turin 1940 – Rome 1994), *Mappa* (1972-73), one of the tapestries made by Afghan embroiderers between 1971 and 1994 to a design by the artist, records the geopolitical state of the world at a specific moment in history, the start of the 1970s, with all of the power relations of the time. The subdivision of the planisphere according to the territorial boundaries for each country, marked by the design of its own flag, highlights the contrast between the artificial system imposed by human beings and the terrestrial shapes created by nature. The text written on the edge of the tapestry integrates the language into the work of art, and contains information on the circumstances of its creation as well as the date and place where it was made. The artist's interest in geography and its political transformations relates these works to the historical scenario that is a part of the artist's favourite themes together with a reflection on time and on the discovery and analysis of the laws and systems governing the world. For Boetti, the very moment of creative conception is a synthesis of the meaning of art-making. The artist renders the thinking process visible through the object-artwork, whose execution can therefore be delegated to other workers.

Alighiero Boetti
Mappa, 1972-73, embroidered by hand on linen, 163 × 217 cm

Gilbert & George
Nothing Breath-Taking Will Occur Here, But..., 1971. Charcoal on paper stretched across a frame, 280 × 225 cm

The four charcoal on paper drawings *As Day Breaks Over Us We Rise Into Our Vacuum, Nothing Breath-Taking Will Occur Here, But..., Our Limbs Begin To Stir And To Form Actions Of Looseness, We Stroll With Specialised Embarrassment And Our Purpose Is Only To Take The Sunshine* are part of a series of 23 that British artists **Gilbert & George** (Gilbert Proesch, San Martino, Bolzano 1943 – George Passmore, Plymouth, Great Britain 1942) made in 1971 entitled *The General Jungle or Carrying on Sculpting*. The drawings are traced from slides taken by the artists while doing a performance in a park in London and projected onto a wall. The work is a sort of transposition of the performance on paper and examines the relationship between natural and artificial, in art as in life, a topic at the very core of the work by the British pair. The iconography cites the tradition of eighteenth-century British landscape painting inspired by the picturesque; the drawing style recalls Vorticism and American Abstract Expressionism. The artists are especially famous for their performances in the 1960s during which, like living sculptures, they would mechanically repeat the same actions for hours on end, against any form of social or cultural convention that shapes individuals. The titles of the 23 drawings, which are really more like captions for the images, are sarcastic commments on the role and utility of the artist in contemporary society.

The image of the sky in the painting *Sternenfall* (1998) by **Anselm Kiefer** (Donaueschingen, Germany 1945) resembles an archive where each star is identified by an alphanumerical code used by NASA to classify celestial bodies. Lines drawn to connect the points design imaginary constellations. Some codes written on glass labels are located on the floor, under the canvas: these are the fallen stars, through which the earth and the sky communicate. At the same time the formal and iconographic comparison with other works by the artist under the title *Sternen-lager* (*Storehouse of Stars*) alludes to German history and particularly the Holocaust. The numbers on the canvas recall those tattooed on the arms of the Jewish prisoners in the Nazi concentration camps. Memory is entwined with the cosmic theme in an indissoluble whole. Art is an instrument that may be used to go back over and transcend history. The redrafting of German cultural tradition exploited for ideological purposes by the Nazi regime, and removed from contemporary German culture is one of the common threads in Kiefer's work alongside the relationship between the microcosm and the macrocosm.

Anselm Kiefer
Sternenfall, 1998, canvas, emulsion, acrylic, shellac, chalk, lead, painted glass, 456 × 530 cm

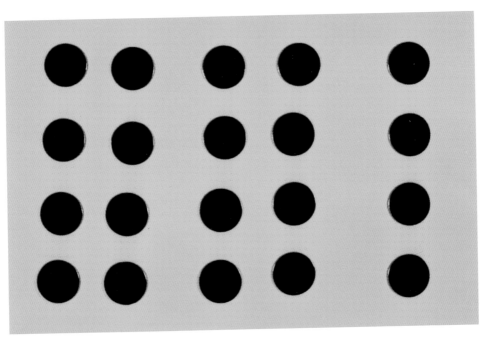

Many of the works from the very rich and heterogeneous artistic production of **Rosemarie Trockel** (Schwerte, Germany 1952) are inspired by the female world. The artist ironically questions the roles historically attributed to sexual genres and the social, political and psychoanalytical theories formulated to justify them. In *Senza Titolo* (2000) twenty electric plates are placed vertically on a painted aluminium base. The geometric volumes, industrial materials and serial nature of the forms all playfully cite Minimalism. The burners located on the wall resemble the canvas of a painting, but they are also potentially dangerous elements which question the figure of the docile, reassuring woman, traditionally at work in the kitchen. At the same time, the passage from the horizontal level, symbolising the female, to a vertical level, referring to the male, releases the object from its practical function and elevates it to aesthetic product.

Rosemarie Trockel
Senza titolo, 2000, pulverized paint on aluminium, 20 electric plates, 172 × 260 × 11.3 cm.
Courtesy Monica Spruth and Philomene Magers.

The three self-portraits by the Finnish artist **Elina Brotherus** (Helsinki 1972) *Femme à sa toilette* (2001), *Le matin* (2001) and *Fille aux fleurs* (2002) are part of the series *The new painting* (2000-04). As compared to her first self-portraits where the photographer examined emotions and episodes in her own life story, such as the death of her parents, marriage and subsequent separation, Brotherus' works in the collection here concentrate on the formal structure of the photographic image rather than on its content. A confrontation with pictorial tradition, especially French Impressionism, is suggested by the titles of the works. The presence of the artist herself as a model for the images, taken by automatic shutter release, is reminiscent of documentary works from the 1960s and 1970s. The purpose of the self-portrait is not to analyse the psychology of the subject, whose face is hidden or out of focus; rather, the figure of the artist is one of the elements in the composition just like the still lifes with vases of flowers in the midst of which she is portrayed in *Fille aux fleurs*.

Elina Brotherus
Fille aux fleurs, 2002, chromogenic print on anodized aluminium, 105 × 130 cm. Courtesy Sonath Gallery, Paris

Francesco Vezzoli
The Kiss (Let's Play Dynasty), 2000,
video, running time 6'

The videos by **Francesco Vezzoli** (Brescia 1971), like his embroidering, are an entwining of the visual material that the artist absorbed while he was growing up: classic cinema (Visconti, Pasolini), literature and theatre, but also the world of television entertainment made up of soap operas, musical videoclips and variety shows. Vezzoli's visual culture mixes and blends fragments and citations from "high" culture with what is considered to be "low" culture. For each of his videos Vezzoli is assisted by the work of professionals from the world of entertainment: authors, set-designers, directors, actors with the goal of assembling a product that complies with the formats featured in television and cinematography. The intention is to emphasise the different genres and their languages by revealing the mechanisms that are being used to communicate. In his video *The Kiss (Let's Play Dynasty)*, 2000, Vezzoli stages an ironic revisitation of the famous American soap opera Dynasty, which is set here, however, in a cultured and refined atmosphere with a hint of homosexuality. The artist himself takes part in it together with Austrian actor Helmut Berger, in an endless game of allusions to and citations from the language of both American television and European cinematography.

Ⓗ GALLERY 2

By taking any one of the paths available you can
continue to walk along Gallery 2, which narrows
until it becomes a catwalk suspended over the
plaza down below. A glass lookout offers a
sudden view of the exterior; it is a pause in the
immersive experience of being inside the
museum. Rather than a building sealed off from
everything else, the MAXXI is an architecture
that is permeable to the surrounding context, a
layering of cantilevered volumes that instil an
osmotic and dynamic relationship with the
exterior: its spaces are the sign and form of an
idea of contemporary culture that is democratic
and participative. The corridor bends to the right
and you are once again inside the main portion
of the building, which leads to Gallery 3.

Giulio Paolini
1/25/71, circa 1971, two
photographs on emulsified canvas,
80 × 182 cm (total dimensions), on
canvas, above left: Giulio Paolini
(1/25/71) 1965-1971

 **GALLERY 3**

This gallery is strongly characterised by the presence of long, knife-like fins in the ceiling that allow the visitor to perceive the variable drift of space. The horizontal plan, interrupted by ramps and balconies at different altitudes, contributes to the unstable and ever-changing nature of this architecture.

Ed Ruscha
I L-Live in H-Hollywood, 1979,
pastel on paper, 58.8 × 73.8 cm

Gallery 3 1,149 sq m

The gallery measures a linear length of 123 m

The height of the roof is 15.80 m

The height of the floor is 9.80 m

⑤

Gallery 3

⑥

View of Gallery 1 from Gallery 3

⑦

Gallery 5 floor

⑧

A permanent installation
by Anish Kapoor is on display
in Gallery 1.

Giuseppe Gabellone
I Giapponesi, 2003, compressed
polyurethane foam, 146 × 103 ×
11 cm. Courtesy Studio Guenzani,
Milan

Ilya and Emilia Kabakov
Where is Our Place?, 2003, installation,
oil on canvas, wood, b/w photographic
prints on paper, fabric, leather, glass,
acrylic on styrofoam, room-size

Francis Alÿs
Sleepers II, 2001, installation,
80 slides, running time 2' 40",
room-size

Nunzio
Avaton, 2007, installation, combusted
wood, 200 × 700 × 160 cm. Courtesy
Galleria dell'Oca, Rome

ⓛ GALLERY 4

Gallery 4, together with Gallery 3, encircles the block of the former Montello barracks. At the far end of the space is a glass lookout onto Via Guido Reni; lifts to the other levels in the building are located to the left.

Gallery 4 1,040 sq m

The gallery measures a linear length of 85 m

A permanent installation by Giuseppe Penone is on display in Gallery 4.

All of the stairways and catwalks suspended over the hall have a support structure that is made up of reticulated beams. The finishing in sheet steel painted black also houses the banister and lighting system. To heighten the effect of lightness and transparency, the floor is a metal grid. Set in the underside of the connecting paths are fluorescent ceiling lights shieded with layers of Barrisol®.

The overall linear development of the stairways measures 160 linear m

The height of the roof is 15.40 m

Ⓜ GALLERY 5

The sequence of exhibition spaces, which has until now been fluid and continuous, ends in Gallery 5, the last one in the museum, with a view on the surrounding urban landscape. The volume, suspended over the plaza at a height of 22.70 m, projects out for a total of 11.60 m. Its tilted floor heightens the sensation of ascent and leap into the void, surprising the visitor, halfway along the path, with a vertiginous glass cut overlooking Gallery 3 underneath.

❶
Gallery 5 758 sq m

❷
The gallery measures a linear length of 55 m

❸
The glass hole in the pavement looks onto Gallery 3 located below

Grazia Toderi
Rosso, 2007, video, loop DVD, projector, DVD player, colour, sound, loop, dimensions variable

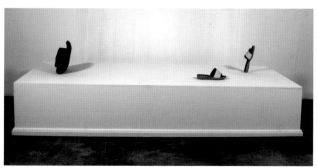

Gino De Dominicis
Statua (Figura distesa), 1979, hat
3 × 4 × 11 cm; woven straw slippers
25 × 9 × 9 cm; wooden base
painted white 40 × 222.6 × 90 cm

Ⓝ EDIFICIO D

Edificio D, made from tufa brickwork with an internal structure in iron constituted by piers and reticulated beams features a number of spaces that may be used for a wide range of activities, the idea being that of adding to what MAXXI has to offer and underscoring its dimension as a mixed-use field project. Ground floor: MAXXI B.A.S.E. (Library, Archives, Studies, Publishing), café, restaurant and bookstore. First floor: the Fondazione MAXXI offices.

During the day the building makes full use of the natural light that filters in through the glass ceiling to guarantee the utmost fruition of the works. At night, the MAXXI lights up like a huge lantern, a brightly lit arabesque that stands out against a view of the city.

All along the plaza the lights in the ground, called turtles, outline the walkways. The bright cathode traces out the contour of the building's perimeter, scenographically illuminating it from below.

Further information

ACTIVITIES AND FACILITIES

MAXXI B.A.S.E. (Library, Archives, Studies, Publishing)

MAXXI B.A.S.E., located in Edificio D, is divided into two sections, one for art and one for architecture, and includes the **Library**, **Media Library**, **Contemporary Archive** and **Photography Archive**. The purpose of the structure is to collect, conserve, create and disseminate the knowledge and culture of contemporary art and architecture, their history, theory, practice and role in today's society. MAXXI B.A.S.E.'s essential role is to document everything that goes on in the museum, from exhibitions to events to scientific activities directly related to the study of the permanent collections. The documentation produced is classified, conserved and made available to the public for consultation. MAXXI B.A.S.E. is a lively and dynamic structure, a research laboratory in every sense of the word. Besides the most important and prestigious international specialised publications, it also features interactive stations, providing the public with avant-garde devices and tools for in-depth research and study into contemporary artistic phenomena. The services offered to the public are integrated with teaching activities, exhibitions and publications. The Contemporary Archive contains all of the museum's holdings, which include a wide range of material – folders, press releases, invitations, posters, photographs, films – all of which available to the public. The Photography Archive is where the visual documentation for the museum's collections and the material used to mount temporary displays is kept.

In the MAXXI, spaces and services are provided that enrich and qualify what both the museum and the city have to offer in terms of culture. The **café** and **restaurant** are dynamic, lively places, truly an extension of the exhibition areas; they are open at night and host cultural events and manifestations that are independent of the museum programme. The **international library** specialising in art, urban studies, design, architecture and photography hosts the finest international publications in the field. Gadgets and other items bearing the MAXXI griffe are available.

Educational Department

The MAXXI's **Educational Department** was founded in 2004, with an agreement to collaborate with the Chair of Didattica del Museo e del Territorio at the Faculty of Scienze Umanistiche, "La Sapienza" University of Rome. Over the years it has experimented with teaching strategies and instruments in temporary exhibitions hosted in Edificio D, developing an integrated methodology for the approach to contemporary art and architecture. A theoretical requirement for the educational programmes offered to children is "learning by doing", assigning great importance to a multisensorial and operative approach that allows for the transmission of the complexity of meanings in contemporary art. The proposals made to the adult public and to families are actual opportunities to meet and learn and they include laboratories, guided visits, workshops with the artists, conferences, dance performances, theatre and concerts. Special attention is paid to what is referred to as the "non-public", that slice of the population that never comes into a museum. Focus groups are set up to understand the reasons for this behaviour and to alter it; research is carried out and then worked on in discussion groups. The project also includes studies carried out by the **Quality Service Office** for the public based on questionnaires, interviews and web-polls; visitor satisfaction is monitored with the goal of continually improving the services offered. Specific proposals are dedicated to visitors who are differently abled or have special needs. A series of experimental projects is aimed at the area's ethnic communities. By introducing a permanent dialogue with such groups the museum can become a special place for exchanges between cultures.

A BIT OF HISTORY

The urban context

Towards the end of the nineteenth century, the area between the Via Flaminia and the ancient Milvio Bridge was a vast stretch of fields that would periodically be flooded by the overflowing of the River Tiber. The first Piano Regolatore (urban development plan) in Rome, dating back to 1909, established that the Flaminio quarter was the ideal place to build plants for industrial production, to which several public housing projects would be added. When the World's Fair was held there a few years later, the area came to be known as a cultural pole for sports entertainment and recreation: the Parioli Race Track, National Stadium, Galleria Nazionale d'Arte Moderna and foreign pavilions were built. Between 1920 and 1940, while plans were being made to build the Foro Mussolini on the opposite shore, a number of projects were being carried out to develop the Flaminio, none of which ever saw the light of day, however. After the Second World War, Rome was chosen to host the Olympics of 1960: the Olympic Village, Palazzetto dello Sport and Stadio Flaminio were built, greatly improving the quarter thanks to the work of Adalberto Libera, Luigi Moretti and Pier Luigi Nervi. When the competition for the new Auditorium was held in 1994, the Flaminio was faced with a third phase of large-scale urban development and, eight years later, the Auditorium Parco delle Musica designed by Renzo Piano was inaugurated, assigning a new role to the area, and introducing the quarter to new ways of experiencing its open spaces.

The former Montello barracks
before the MAXXI, view from
Via Masaccio

The former Montello barracks,
interior of one of the pavilions

The competition and the museum's earliest events

In 1997, a proposal was launched by the Italian Ministry of Culture to build a great new national district for contemporary art and architecture and to locate it in the Flaminio quarter in Rome. In the autumn of the same year, the Ministry of Defence relinquished ownership of what was formerly the Montello army barracks.

The following year an international competition was held calling for ideas for the development of a National Contemporary Arts Centre: the two-phased competition witnessed entries by 273 candidates; 15 semi-finalists were selected by a jury and allowed to take part in the second phase of the competition. In late February 1999, the jury chose the project put forward by the Iraqi-born, London-based architect Zaha Hadid, and at the end of the following year work began on the Centre for Contemporary Art. The first foundation stone was laid in the presence of the authorities in 2003. Work began on the new Centre, whose new name was MAXXI_Museo nazionale delle arti del XXI secolo. While work was being done to finish the complex, Edificio D, the portion of the ex-barracks that has been left to adjoin the museum's new spaces, was refurbished and transformed into a temporary exhibition area. The MAXXI opened to the public on May 30, 2010.

The 15 semi-finalists
• Adam Caruso, Peter St. John (Great Britain)
• Francesco Cellini, Franco Ceschi (Italy)
• Michele De Lucchi, Achille Castiglioni, Italo Lupi (Italy)
• Eduardo Souto de Moura (Portugal)
• Vittorio Gregotti, Franco Purini (Italy)
• Zaha Hadid (Great Britain)
• Steven Holl, Guy Nordenson (United States)
• Toyo Ito (Japan)
• OMA – Rem Koolhaas (Netherlands)
• Pierluigi Nicolin, Italo Rota (Italy)
• Jean Nouvel (France)
• Christos Papoulias (Greece)
• Mosè Ricci, Carmen Andriani, Aldo Aymonino, Pippo Ciorra, Filippo Spaini (Italy)
• SANAA – Kazuyo Sejima, Ryue Nishizawa (Japan)
• Cino Zucchi, Stefano Boeri (Italy)

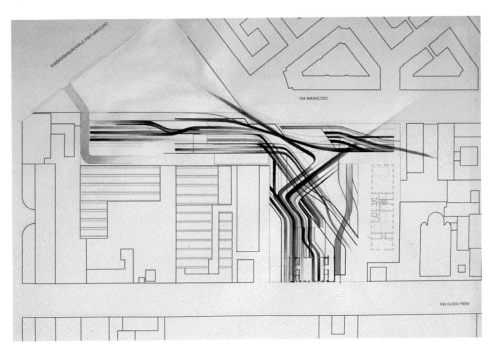

Zaha Hadid
Competition entry, setting in the
urban context

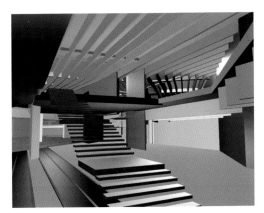

Zaha Hadid
Competition entry, digital rendering
of interior

The project

Zaha Hadid's project cut the block diagonally, tracing a pedestrian axis that defines the form of the main building. The crossing is at the same time a plaza and an open-air display. Designed so that it would closely relate to the museum, this promenade offers the passers-by views, unexpected connections and new opportunities for the community life of the neighbourhood and in Rome. The museum's winding masses represent a new presence on the urban scene. The exhibition complex makes a very definite mark that delimits and surrounds the exterior, with cantilevered volumes that act as a counterpoint to the more sober interiors of the galleries destined to host the collections for the two museums. The latter are distinguished by their different degrees of permeability, flexibility and transparency. The interior is not just a linear route, rather, it offers its visitors opportunities for alternative visits, allowing users to personalise their paths, with evocative views of the architecture, the works on display and the city, in a continual osmosis between interior and exterior.

Zaha Hadid
Competition entry, painting

The construction site

The MAXXI's construction site was the occasion for experimentation and technical-constructive innovation. The shape of the building, the materials and the way they were put to use have turned this realisation into a unique experience where form and structure coincide. The structural planning of the building could never have been achieved without the complex three-dimensional digital renderings that allowed for measurement of the building's load distribution and deformation. Huge, single pourings of concrete, some even 60 metres long and 9 metres high, achieved continuous and uniform surfaces, with no openings and no signs of construction. This required the use of a new mix of concrete, as well as special formworks with non-standard sizes and a specially finished surface. The project for the MAXXI might be seen as a compendium of all of the possible declensions for concrete, for it is used in almost every single part of the complex, including the floors. Although it might be defined a kind of "low-technology", widely used for its easy versatility, concrete actually combines quite well with the concept of "flux" that Zaha Hadid raised to levels of extreme formal expressiveness in this project.

MAXXI, view of the construction site

Bibliography and websites

Dalle armi alle arti. Trasformazioni e nuove funzioni urbane nel quartiere Flaminio, edited by A. Vittorini, Gangemi Editore, Rome 2004.
MAXXI - Museo nazionale delle arti del XXI secolo, edited by P. Baldi, Electa OperaDarc, Milan 2006.
Zaha Hadid, by M. Guccione, Federico Motta Editore, Milan 2007.
Galleria Nazionale d'arte moderna & MAXXI, Le collezioni 1958-2008, edited by S. Frezzotti, C. Italiano, A. Rorro, Electa, Milan 2009.
Materia grigia, edited by M. Avagnina, M. Guccione, S. La Pergola, Electa, Milan 2010.
MAXXI Architettura. Collezioni di fotografia, edited by F. Fabiani, Electa, Milan 2010.
Spazio, dalle collezioni di arte e architettura del MAXXI, edited by S. Chiodi and D. Dardi, Electa, Milan 2010.

www.maxxi.beniculturali.it

MAXXI library online catalogue:
http://opac.uniroma1.it/SebinaOpacR
MS/Opacsysb=RMSMX.